A CUP OF INSPIRATION

Reviving Your Soul
in Twenty-One Sips

Vol. 1

A CUP OF INSPIRATION

Reviving Your Soul in Twenty-One Sips

VOL. 1

CEITCI DEMIRKOVA

CEITCI DEMIRKOVA MINISTRIES

Dedication

This book is dedicated to my Lord and best friend Jesus, who has captured my heart by His love. He is my inspiration and my passion.

Introduction

Have you ever asked yourself the question, "What kind of ingredients 'supply' the motion to my ideas and goals in life?" Personally, I believe that words play the most essential role in starting and carrying out a vision for a specific task. Words equal power, both positive and negative, depending on the situation in which they are used. One spoken word can build or destroy hope; one word can inspire and motivate, or bring fear and discouragement.

After seeing an incredible film, it's very possible to feel that you too could one day be just like the hero you watched. The words of inspiration that accompany pictures and actions can suddenly inject you with new energy and hope. The circumstances around you might be the same, the fears might seem more real than the miracle, and the impossibility much greater than what you can handle, but once your spirit, and your mind, have encountered and embraced words of inspiration, a new action is underway.

Every one of the articles in this 21-day devotional book describes a time of my life when just "one word" from the right source was the saving rope to carry me out of devastation into victory. That "one word" was and still is the Word of God. When spoken by Christ, "one word" transforms, revives, brings hope, changes circumstances, and inspires you to keep on going.

A Cup of Inspiration reaches into God's well, the Bible, and offers you a taste of the living water. Once you try it, you will never want to stop drinking.

May you always thirst after God, the One who is our ultimate inspiration, and whose "cup" of promises overflows every day of our lives!

Still drinking from The Well,

Ceitci Demirkova

Ceitci Demirkova

∼∼∼ DAY I ∼∼∼

Do you believe in the God of today?

John 11:1-44

Unstoppable tears of pain and agony rolled down the faces of Mary and Martha. It seemed as though the dark, cold cave had swallowed the body of their brother Lazarus, leaving only memories of his presence. The big stone covering the cave's entrance was now still. Their feelings were surreal; their minds were incapable of comprehending the shocking tragedy that uninvitingly had invaded their family. Thoughts of panic rose, trying to find a place of refuge beyond the questions of their souls. Tears couldn't wash away the pain that was leaving gashes of anguish deep in their hearts. If only Jesus had been there, their brother would not have died. This was more than just another idle thought. Their sorrow demanded an answer.

Without trying to hide her tender wounds and disappointment at the absence of Jesus' presence during her brother's final hours, Martha approached Jesus. He was entering Bethany, but four days too late. However, hope and faith rekindled in Martha's heart. "But even now I know that whatever You ask of God, God will give You," she said to her Lord.

"Your brother will rise again...I am the resurrection and the life. He who believes in Me, though he may die, he shall live. And whoever lives and believes in Me shall never die. Do you believe this?"

The question pierced her heart. She remembered what Jesus had done. She also knew what He would do one day when He returned, but did she have faith to believe that He could resurrect her brother today?

Jesus was not looking for another answer from Martha. He was looking for faith. "Naked faith" I like to call it—uncovered humanness that hides in the greatness of God's unchanging character and power. It is the kind of faith that doesn't just believe a promise, but believes in the God who gave the promise; it is faith that doesn't pretend or boast in the knowledge of the scriptures, but abides in the presence of the One who gave His Word.

Jesus is asking us the same question today He asked Martha years ago: "Do you believe in Me today?" Not, "Did you believe in My miracles yesterday?" or, "Do you think that one day I will perform this miracle?" but, "Do you believe today? Or am I too late for your problem and impossibility?"

Perhaps it's been four days, four years, or over a decade. How late is too late, when the God of Resurrection comes to your rescue? Are we afraid of being theologically incorrect by believing in God's promises given to us for today?

The kind of naked faith that Jesus is looking for is greater than human logic, religious doctrine, or any other man-made spiritual philosophy. Jesus waits until it's humanly impossible for you and me to unroll the stones that have kept our promises in a cold, dark cave. He waits until we have come to the end of our rope, and all that is left is us and Him. When everyone and everything has been removed and stripped from us and only Jesus is standing before us. There is no one else to run, and no one else to hug—just Christ. That very moment becomes our miracle.

"Come forth!" He says.

Our tears have been dried, our desires have been fulfilled, and our promises have been resurrected, but most importantly, we have allowed ourselves to believe again, to believe in Jesus today.

⤜⤏ DAY 2 ⤍⤛

How close is close enough?

"For she said to herself 'If only I may touch His clothes, I shall be made well.'" (Mark 5:28)

The negative doctors' reports she had heard for twelve years, the hypercritical looks from her relatives and neighbors, combined with the ongoing pain in her body now served as a motivation to press through the multitude of people, rather than stand behind in despair. One look at Jesus was enough to trigger a glimmer of hope in her that somehow life would be revived within her incurable body. With eyes locked on Him, pulling all of her strength together, she pressed once again through the crowd. Almost there! Christ seemed so close. She could see Him walking slowly ahead, but was still not close enough to be seen by Him. "I will be made whole," she repeated to herself, "if I can only touch His garment." Her weak body ached as she pulled herself through the crowd and stretched forth her hand in a final attempt. In an instant, barely touching Jesus' clothes, she felt healing flow through her body. The fountain of her blood dried up, and she was free from the bondage of her sickness. A calming peace and a sense of excitement came over her, till she heard Jesus say,

"Who touched my clothes?" Oh, no! Was Jesus mad? Did He know it was her? Why did it matter?

Trying to hide her shame, with trembling she fell before His feet and told Him the truth. Her fear was visible; her broken heart was fully uncovered before the eyes of the Creator. It seemed as though time stopped when Jesus looked into the depth of her soul and validated her dignity, her womanhood, and her faith in God in front of all who were watching, by saying, "Daughter, your faith has made you well. Go in peace, and be healed of your affliction." His words did not convey condemnation, but new life, affirmation, and love. Jesus knew that, above all, the woman who touched Him needed not only physical healing, as she thought, but also eternal salvation and emotional restoration.

In the midst of the pressure from the multitude, Jesus stopped to look and speak to the one – the one who believed in Him; the one who didn't let the crowd defer her focus; the one who came close enough to catch His attention with her faith.

Perhaps at times we have felt as though the "crowds" around us are not giving us adequate space to approach Jesus. Somehow, the pressure of work, family affairs, impossible circumstances, and our need for healing or provision can pull us away from the presence of Jesus. We can see Him, yet can't fully reach Him because there is a "crowd" separating us. When you find yourself stuck in the crowd, look for Jesus. Keep your focus on Him, and let your faith rise above the natural "crowds" in your life. Their pressures and impossibilities do not influence Christ. He knows the way; the "crowd" only follows. "How close is close enough?" - When we touch Jesus and are transformed in His presence.

~~~ DAY 3 ~~~

High Impact

As I held my street directions in one hand, moving slowly in traffic, I glanced out the right window of my silver rental car. The big city of New York seemed to glow in the reflection of the sun. There is an illusion that all of New York City is inviting and full of excitement. However, danger lies hidden in the dark streets and corners of the inner city of Brooklyn, NY that could never be sensed from driving on the highways and bridges of the city.

I soon approached an area in Brooklyn that most taxis avoid. The picture of the inner city is painted by gangs, drugs, shootings, homeless people, and street children. It is definitely not on the list of tourist attractions. Coming from a former Communist country, it seems impossible to think that even in America exist places that can be considered "third world" in nature.

I finally arrived at my destination: Metro International Ministries. Even though I had been there three times before, I still found myself asking the question, "What would make someone risk their life to bring the Gospel to the people of the Bronx?" From Metro Ministries I have learned that the driving force of any impact is commitment. Commitment gives us the courage to face danger or pay whatever cost required to make an impact!

I want to challenge you today to break out of your ordinary routine and allow your commitment to the Gospel to motivate you to make an impact for eternity. We have come to believe that only a big action produces big results. However, that is not what Jesus requires. He only asks for obedience. Big commitment equals daily obedience to His voice. Daily obedience creates a great impact on those around us, an impact motivated out of our love and commitment to Him!

❧ ☞ DAY 4 ☜❧

The breath of life

Psalms 121:1-2

Close your eyes for just a moment and imagine yourself running down a hill as a little child, pulling a kite behind you. Your heartbeat increases as you accelerate downward. The kite's string grows taut in your hand, urging you to join it in flight. It's time. You release control. Tiredness disappears and your heart charges with excitement as you watch the kite soar into the blue skies. That same kite was lying in a box, lifeless and still, just an hour ago. What makes it so animated now? We all know the answer—it's simple—it's called wind. The current of the air becomes the breath of life for a motionless kite.

As I have observed my life and the lives of those around me, I have noticed how easy it is for problems, betrayals, sickness, and disappointments to knock the wind out of us. Somehow life itself has a way of getting us off course and often even facing the wrong direction. Could it be that what once seemed alive in our hearts now lies dormant and frozen in past memories?

I would like to remind you of the wind of God. It's a wind that has power to quicken life into dead bodies, into dead hearts, and into dead dreams. God desires to breathe back into us new vision, new excitement, and new purpose. Examine the areas of your heart that are not fully alive. Don't be afraid. Ask God to revive them. He has given us His Holy Spirit. He is our breath of life. Jesus said that He will be "our Teacher, our Guide, and our Comforter."

Imagine yourself letting go of the kite string. You release control. This time though, it's not the kite, it's you! The wind of God breathes His life into you and you become fully alive.

"I will lift up my eyes to the hills—from whence comes my help? My help comes from the Lord, who made heavens and earth." Psalms 121:1-2

☕ ➤ DAY 5 ☜

Our Refuge

Psalms 91:1-2

It's early afternoon. The sun rays are gradually making their way through the white puffy clouds. The ocean is nearly calm; only small, short waves formed by a light breeze run onto the shore as though looking for escape. Thousands of black stones in different shapes scattered along the shore give spice to the sandy beach. The mountain tops, still covered in snow, are beginning to glow radiantly as the sun uncovers its round, shining face upon them.

The wind, ceasing for a split second, makes nature's beauty even more intriguing and breathtaking. God's magnificence and His never-ending creativity reveal to us His goodness and nature. He is in love with us, with you and me.

As the day progresses, the wind returns, empowering and transforming the water into a boisterous mass of waves. A short hiking trail leads to the top of a hill overlooking the ocean and the mountains. Once there, you feel as though you have entered a different world. The trees standing tall, lined up side by side, do not allow the wind to penetrate the peace.

The birds are still singing and the sun is still shining over the mountaintop. The beautiful ocean is visible through the tree branches at the edge of the hill. Even though you can hear the whisper of the wind, you can barely feel it. Somehow, the furious waves seem to have disappeared. From this distance your perspective has changed. Everything else is the same, but you have reached a higher level!

When the storms of life begin to rage around you, remember to change your elevation. Climb high into His presence! Only one minute with Him will change your entire viewpoint on life. God specializes in miracles. He doesn't necessarily calm the storm, but He provides sanctuary for you in the palm of His hand while you walk through it. The wind is still there, but it can't harm you because you have been sheltered. God takes you to a higher level, and puts "the glasses of faith" on your eyes. The crashing waves have disappeared, and the Son's rays are now shining upon you. You are His creation, showing forth His goodness. He is in love with you!

<del>☜ DAY 6 ☞</del>

Walking the desert

Book of Ruth

Desert and wilderness are perhaps not the most favorite words in our Christian vocabulary. However, deserts are not unfamiliar places for most of us. No matter how far we come in our Christian walk, at one point or another we have to pass through a desert.

Speaking in geographical terms, deserts are barren, arid places with no noticeable vegetation or water supply. This translates into a significant spiritual metaphor. When joy and peace are absent, and our enthusiasm for life is gone, these are the times that we call "spiritual barrenness" or "wilderness."

Without understanding the purpose behind every desert in our lives, we could easily get sidetracked, discouraged, or walk in circles just like the children of Israel.

In recent studies of the book of Ruth, I came to realize that in order for Ruth and Naomi to change history and to fulfill God's destiny for their lives, they had to go through the desert. Naomi left the land of Moab and returned to Judah. She went back to her native land in order for God to restore her life after many years of disobedience. Ruth, on the other hand, completely devoted to her mother-in-law, left the familiar and entered into the redemptive plan of God for her life.

Here we see two women in action: one moving backwards in order to change the past, the other moving forward so that she could influence the future. The desert stretched between the past and the future. They had no other choice but to go through it. If they had faced the desert without purpose, they would have died. Their vision and determination kept them alive.

Journeying through the "deserts" of our lives leads us to understand with greater measure the unfailing love of our God. The spiritual deserts strip from us our false identity in order to find ourselves clothed in His righteousness. Their purpose is to take away everything that we rely upon in order to make God our only source and vision. The desert is not for our harm; rather it is a place of preparation for our Promised Land.

Some of our greatest victories and blessings flow out of our "desert time experiences." It's up to us to change our outlook, and to begin to walk "the desert" with purpose!

⋐⋙ DAY 7 ⋘⋙

A leader with a "Different Spirit"

"But My servant Caleb, because he has a different spirit in him and has followed Me fully, I will bring into the land where he went, and his descendants shall inherit it."

Numbers 14:24

We live in a time of urgency when God is looking for true leaders, both men and women, who are not afraid to rise up with courage and boldness and proclaim the Word of the Lord. In the midst of immorality, religious rituals, and deception, our Lord is requiring us to influence the spiritual climate and lift up a new standard in the land. Every one of us has "a land" that must be occupied for Christ. Ask yourself who represents your land. It could be your family, your friends, your neighbors, or impossibilities and circumstances. The fact is that those who dwell in our "Future Promised Land" need to know that we are not afraid to walk by faith when the ground underneath our feet seems unstable, and that we are not ashamed to stand up for what is godly and righteous.

Joshua and Caleb are two examples from the Old Testament who believed God's promises and were willing to obey the Lord, even in the face of great opposition. Numbers 14:24 describes Caleb as a servant with a "different spirit." The word different used in this passage captured my attention. It reveals the fact that Caleb and Joshua were willing to sacrifice their reputation and position among men in order to accept the one given to them by the Lord. They were leaders appointed by God, who arose with faith in a time of need and desperation.

God had promised the children of Israel the land of Canaan, but they had to go in and possess it. Because of the giants dwelling in the land, the spies who were sent in came back and gave the people a negative and fearful report. Joshua and Caleb were the only two who saw beyond the natural dangers and into the promise God had made. Together, with those who believed in their report and followed them, they inherited the Promised Land.

There are three things that are admirable about both of these men. First, they obeyed God rather than man. Second, they were not seeking to be popular or to win people over to their side. In fact, not many were for them, but that didn't discourage them. Love motivated them to compel the Israelites to remember God's miracles and His promises. Third, they didn't boast in themselves, but gave God the praise and glory. God has called you and me to be people who have that "different" spirit inside of us. May we all become leaders who take the challenges of life and lead others into the promises of God as we lay down our lives and lead out of God's love!

∼ DAY 8 ∼

The missing piece

The message of Spiritual destiny is becoming more and more alive in me. While recently preparing for a service, I had a vision of an army of soldiers going to the battlefield. Some of them had their armor and weapons on, but were sitting down and resting, while the rest of the army was getting mad for doing their job and complaining about it. The war had started, but most of them were not fighting, they were hiding.

How could that picture exemplify a spiritual abstract? Simply. Many people in the body of Christ have not taken their place as soldiers in God's army. Therefore some do the "extra" work, and some just wait for the battle to be over. Believe it or not, we are engaged in a spiritual war and we all have a role to fill. There are things that God has predestined for each of us to do and no one else can accomplish our task for us. We must step and fill in the empty place in the big puzzle. There is a part that only you can play in changing this world, and unless you do it, this place remains empty.

God spoke to Jeremiah in Jeremiah 1:6-10, saying that He had called him before he was even born and he just had to say "Yes" to the destiny God had preordained for him. Because of Jeremiah's fear, God reassured him that he would be with him. He touched his mouth in verses 9-10, and as a result Jeremiah, spoke prophetically all that God revealed to him. God's words in his mouth were all the authority he needed to do the work that God had called him to do.

You have that same kind of authority. When you have the Word of God inside of you, you have everything you need to overcome every situation or problem that comes against you. (Mark 16:17 and Acts 1:8). Don't wait for someone else to act, but stand up and take your place in the body of Christ. Don't ever let God's Word depart from your mouth, but fill yourself up with it and let it come out like a mighty sword dividing the truth from the lies of the enemy.

You have a job to do and God is counting on you!

DAY 9

"Then it shall be to Me a name of joy..."

Jeremiah 33:9

During one of my prayer times, God placed a special verse on my heart. It was Jeremiah 33:3, which states, "Call unto Me and I will show you great and mighty things, which you don't know." Even though this is a familiar passage of scripture, I believe very few of us have actually experienced the promises within that verse.

The particular word "call" describes calling out loud, getting someone's attention, or giving someone a name. In Genesis 29:32 Leah bore a son and said, "Now I will praise the Lord," and she called his name Judah, which means "praise." Out of Judah through David came Jesus, who praised and glorified the Father in all that He did.

Every day we are in situations when we need to get the attention of another person. The appropriate way of doing that is by calling out their first or last name. If they hear their name called out, they respond back. The same applies when we call upon the Lord. We are to call Him according to the name we would like for Him to answer us! For example, when we need healing we are to call Him Jehovah Rapha, our

Healer; when we need provision, we are to call Him Jehovah Jireh, our Provider. According to the names we call Him, He promises to show us great and mighty things that reveal His nature in a personal way.

The interesting part about this verse is hidden in the word "mighty," meaning "a revelational insight." When we combine the meanings of these words, we come to understand that when we call God our Savior, our Deliverer, our Father, our Banner, our Advocate, etc., only then will He give us a revelational insight of who He is and what He can do.

We need to have a revelation of who God is in order to believe what He says. Chapter 33 of Jeremiah discusses the restored nation of Israel. Today, we can also experience God's promise of restoration and hope, but first we are to call upon Him and "Then it shall be to Me a name of joy, a praise and an honor before all nations of the earth, who shall hear all the good that I do for them; they shall fear and tremble for all the goodness and all the prosperity that I provide for it" (Jeremiah 33:9). The word "it" means you and I! You can put your name every time you see "it" in the verse and declare it as a promise God has made to you. You will be to Him a name of joy, of praise, and of honor before all nations of the earth, when you call upon Him.

ᐸᕤᕝ DAY 10 ᐸᕤᕝ

Is there not a cause?

1 Samuel 17

Great fear filled the hearts of King Saul and all Israel when they heard that a Philistine by the name of Goliath was coming to fight them. Even though Goliath was only a man, his stature exceeded six cubits and a span (nine feet and nine inches). He was full of hate and anger towards God's people and was very confident in his strength to defeat anyone brave enough to fight him. Out of all the trained warriors in Israel, there was not one willing to fight the giant.

Terror began to escalate among the people as the day of the fight drew near. In the midst of the crisis, however, God had already made a provision for deliverance. He had chosen a shepherd boy, by the name of David, who would defeat Goliath. David was young, unskilled, and appeared to be unqualified to fight. His heart, however, was full of confidence in God and there was no hint of fear as he accepted Goliath's challenge. When his brothers tried to discourage him from entering the battlefield, David asked, "Is there not a cause?"

To everyone else, even his own family, David was only a child, but in the eyes of God he was already a mighty warrior and a king. His confidence to stand up against Goliath came from the realization that he would not be fighting a battle for his own glory, but a victory that must be won so that others "might live." David was secure in the covenant relationship he had with God, and therefore he was able to boldly speak God's word in the face of the Philistine: "I come to you in the name of the Lord of hosts, the God of the armies of Israel, whom you have defied."

We live in a history-making time. It's very important that we stay alert and allow only God's word to be our guide and our weapon in times of battle. We all have different "giants" that we face. The question is not, "Should I fight?" but rather, "Is there not a cause?" When we come into agreement with the lies of the enemy, fear will grip our hearts. The giant you are facing is not in a covenant relationship with our God; you are! For that reason alone, you have already won the battle ahead of you!

"Is there not a cause?" Yes, there is! It's not about us, but about people. It's so that others might see that when one person takes a stand and speaks God's word, it is the Lord who fights the battle and brings forth supernatural victory!

DAY II

Staying focused

Philippians 3:14

In all that we do here on the earth, we have to know that what we are doing is for Jesus. He is the author and the finisher of our faith. He is the greatest example we need to follow. You and I were on His mind when He went to the cross. The shame and rejection He endured was not so that He could show us that He is God, but because He loved us. The ones who have lived before us and are now in heaven have left a witness and an example we can follow. If they made it, so can we. Almost every verse of Hebrews chapter 11 starts with the words, "By faith..." It was by faith that Abraham and everyone else after him inherited the promises of God. They had a race to run and a destiny to fulfill, but they had to remain focused on the finish line.

When I was in college, I went repelling on the face of a cliff in Oklahoma. I was surrounded by friends who encouraged me and cheered me on. Knowing that the key to repelling was to relax and allow the rope to grab my weight, I allowed myself to trust my equipment and my instincts. During this life-changing experience, I learned an important lesson in focus. While repelling you can't look in any other direction than up. Similarly, when you and I are called by God to do His will, focusing on Jesus is what will keep us from getting sidetracked.

When I finally got down the cliff, I couldn't boast in myself, because if the people holding the rope had not been in the right place doing the right things, I never would have been successful. Jesus is the rope that supports us and holds us, but we have to release our control and go with the flow of His timing.

In Philippians 3:14, Paul encourages us not to lose sight of the goals that God has set before us. "I press on toward the goal to win the prize for which God has called me heavenward in Christ Jesus." When you are staring at the cliff, remember to look up and trust that He's your rope.

๑ ๛ DAY 12 ๑๛

The Cross is waiting

John 19

The voice of the crowd resounded as though one person was yelling with anger, full of hatred and judgment: "Away with Him, away with Him! Crucify Him!" And the order was given. On a cold and barren hill, called Golgotha, God placed His only Son on a rugged cross and offered Him as a sacrifice for the redemption of humankind. Our sins became the nails in His hands and feet, forcefully binding our corrupt identity, our guilt, our wrongdoings, our shame, our pride, our pain, and our sickness into the nature of the One who knew no sin. Those "nails" remained until Christ was fully permeated with every possible sin that you and I ever have done or ever could do.

The Father took His Son and broke His body, and the contents of flesh and blood were poured out, cleansing us from all unrighteousness, and opening a new door into a permanent relationship with our Creator. Through the resurrection of Christ, the Father made His Son a living cross, saturating our humanity with His love and acceptance for eternity. That Cross stands to this day outside of the gates of religiosity, tradition, and people's opinions. His arms are stretched wide and His feet stand firm, offering us free access to come! For those who encounter the Cross for the first time, He is Salvation! Once saved through Him we have one more decision to make: are we willing to pay the price and pick up the Cross and bring Him inside, to the places where we live, where we work, where we relax, so that those who still live inside of the "gates" have the opportunity to meet Him?

The Cross is usually associated with nails, pain and death, but let's not forget that only after death is there resurrection. After death there is power! After death there is victory! After death there is new life! The "nails" in our hands and in our feet could represent the challenges, the impossibilities, the false accusations, the pain, and the unfairness life brings. Yet, those are only temporary, binding us closer to Christ until His nature permeates every part of our being. Only then we can experience His full resurrection—dead to our sin, our will, and our pride, yet alive in Christ!

My prayer today in writing this article is that you might receive a greater revelation of the Cross, and that the words in Galatians 2:20 might become a part of your life: "I have been crucified with Christ; it's no longer I who live, but Christ lives in me; and the life which I now live in the flesh I live by faith in the Son of God, who loved me and gave Himself for me." (Galatians 2:20)

⤳ ⤳ DAY 13 ⤳⤳

His Passion—Our Redemption

pas·sion (păsh' æn) n. **1.** often capitalized
a. The sufferings of Christ between the night of
the Last Supper and His death
b. An oratorio based on a gospel narrative of
the Passion. [Middle English, from Old French,
from Late Latin passio, suffering, being acted
upon, from Latin pati, to suffer.]

Rolling dark clouds swelled in the relentless wind. It
was a day like no other. Blood was streaming down
from the cross onto the stony ground. Terrified,
astonished, and covered in a blanket of fear, the
hearts of those remaining around the cross stood
frozen. With a loud voice, Jesus cried out again, and
gave up His spirit. In one instant, darkness overcame
light, fear overtook peace, and hatred overtook love,
giving Satan an illusive victory. Then, just as he
thought of triumph, the earth shook, rocks split, and
the curtain of the temple was torn in two.

The plan that God had started with creation came to
its final realization through the death and resurrection
of Jesus Christ. With every tremor from the earth on
that day, God was proclaiming out loud the final
defeat of Satan. Righteousness prevailed over

injustice, love was victorious over fear, and Christ's redemption defeated Satan's deception.

Christ came with a vision, He lived with a purpose, and He died with a passion. Even Webster's Dictionary gives us a primary description of the word, passion by using Jesus' sufferings as an example. His passion brought our redemption, and His resurrection brought complete restoration of our lost relationship with God.

The same power which shook the earth, the same Spirit that resurrected Jesus from the dead, and the same God, who is passionately in love with us, empowers us today to live out His plan here on the earth.

Each day of our lives we have an opportunity to celebrate the resurrection of Jesus Christ. Let us continuously remember— His passion that drew Him to the cross was for you, and for me. His Passion = Our Redemption!

DAY 14

From the heart

I remember listening to a sermon about a year ago which discussed the urgency of the hour in which we are living. A particular phrase stuck in my mind. Since then, on many occasions, before or after I minister, those words rush back to my mind: "Once you touch Jesus' wounds, you can never be the same." Even to this day, my heart jumps when I remember that statement. It awakens in me a desire to do more for Jesus than ever before in my life.

For over two years God has been taking me on a different route; perhaps harder or more challenging at times, but one definitely worth traveling. Ministering, and helping people spiritually as well as financially, have always been a part of my vision and the purpose of my ministry. Yet, these things never would have happened if I had not allowed Christ to come close enough to me to hear His heart beat and touch His wounds. The phrase to which I am referring comes from John 20:27-28. Thomas wasn't sure if Jesus was really raised, even though He was standing in front of him. His doubts stemmed from one desire—to know the truth. Unlike many of us, he acknowledged his doubt and allowed Jesus to bring him to belief. Touching Jesus' wounds brought not only confirmation but also eternal transformation in Thomas. What do I mean by that?

We will never be effective enough to reach the end of the "race set before us" unless we make up our minds to come close enough to Jesus to feel His wounds. He was nailed and pierced for us. Those wounds still bleed for those who don't know Him. Every single time we touch a person's life, we touch the wounds of Christ.

That is why I can't get tired of preaching, praying, or giving out what God has given me. Once you come close enough to Jesus, it's too late to go back and be the same! The key is: Even when Thomas didn't believe, Jesus believed in him and loved him.

Jesus believes in you! Once you have that revelation it doesn't take much to get started. Once you touch His wounds you are qualified to go!

～✦ DAY 15 ✦～

Inscribed on the palm of His hand

It was about 8:00 p.m. when we arrived at the Brooklyn Bridge for a prayer walk over New York City and America. I was part of the last Metro Boot Camp program for the spring session of the year.

Our group consisted of about thirty people from across America who had come for a week to Brooklyn, NY, to embrace a vision of how to reach their cities. This particular evening was only our third night together, but all of us felt as though we had known each other for months. In less than three days we were a part of many group activities, a rope's course, Sidewalk Sunday School, blitzing on the streets in the inner city, as well as visitation to the homes of the children who attended Sunday school. Even though our group consisted of people from different churches, denominations, and backgrounds, the vision to reach out and save the lives of the inner city children had brought all of us to a place of unity and purpose.

While walking on the bridge, looking at the buildings, the cars driving below us, and the people passing by, I stopped to take a picture. Pretty far away I spotted the Stature of Liberty. Though she seemed small from such a distance, she still symbolized the freedom

America is known for. Many memories rushed back into my mind. It seemed like yesterday that I boarded an airplane for the first time in my life and flew from Bulgaria to the United States. New York City was my first destination in the country. I still remember looking through the small glass window of the plane as we circled right above that same Stature of Liberty. All of the skyscrapers were dazzling with lights, and New York City appeared picture perfect, just as I had seen it in movies.

It's been a little bit over ten years since I first stepped on American soil at the JFK International Airport. I had just turned nineteen years old, and my heart was full of excitement and mixed expectations of what my "new life" would be like. At that time I didn't know many people, didn't have much money, and didn't even speak English fluently. Little did I know that one day I would be standing on the Brooklyn Bridge praying for America, ministering in the inner city, and traveling full time across the country—preaching the Gospel.

As I stood on the bridge, my heart was filled with gratitude to God for His faithfulness and love. He had exceeded my expectations and desires. Isaiah 49:16 came to my mind: "See, I have inscribed you on the palms of My hands; Your walls are continually before Me."

God loves and desires each one of us so much that He has inscribed our names on the palms of His hands. A lasting record has been made, describing specifically what His plan is for your life and mine.

Times come when the cares of life overwhelm our minds. Those moments give us an opportunity to remember that because God's plan for our lives is laid out, obstacles, people, governments, and mistakes cannot stop that plan from coming to pass. It helps us to trust the Lord even during the hard times when things don't make sense. When we know that we have been inscribed on the palm of His hands we can relax and give Him the control and power to form us according to His plan and lead us where He desires.

My prayer is that we all would have a revelation of this simple truth: God is for us! We are continuously on His mind and nothing can separate us from His love, because we have been inscribed on the palm of His hands.

ᕯᕷᕿ DAY 16 ᕯᕷᕿ

The power of a choice

John 10:17-18

The lights were dim, and the people sat reverently in the pews as a worship band finished their last song. Not even a few minutes into the silence that ensued, the back door of the church opened and a local policeman walked in. His strong, raspy voice pierced the quietness. "A new law has been passed today requiring all Christians to submit their Bibles to the local police stations," he shouted. "Everyone who is not willing to participate will be subject to a mandatory jail sentence." While still talking, he made his way toward the front, stood before the pastor and demanded that he be the first to deny Christ by submitting his Bible. The congregation watched in disbelief. How could this be happening in the United States?

I witnessed this dramatization while I was speaking at a youth conference in Louisiana (June 2004) where I shared about my life under Communism. Even though I was never taken to jail in Bulgaria because of my faith, the above portrayal was, and still is, a part of normal life in many parts of the world. People are faced daily with the decision to choose Christ or to deny Him. For them, it's not a drama; it's a life or death decision. The Christians in this situation seem to know that when they say "Yes" to Christ they are choosing life that cannot be taken away from them by man-made law.

According to Webster's Dictionary, to "choose" is to "select freely after consideration." Choice requires the activation of will power. Laws cannot take away our will power. Laws cannot force or prevent us from loving Christ. Choice is a very powerful ability! God has given us a will and the power to choose; it is our nature because we are made in His image. Since we bear His image, we have the ability to choose life, freedom, love, hope, acceptance, and peace—even when circumstances around us seem to dictate otherwise. Negative external events cannot enslave our internal being when we discover the power of choice! Be encouraged today as you choose Christ— celebrate your freedom to choose as you remember the One who freely chose to give His life for you.

"Therefore My Father loves Me, because I lay down My life that I may take it again. No one takes it from Me, but I lay it down of Myself. I have power to lay it down, and I have power to take it again. This command I have received from My Father." John 10:17-18

~~~ DAY 17 ~~~

A Christmas I will never forget

Testimony

We never know how valuable life is until we are faced with death. During one of my Christmases in America, I was given a second chance to live. I decided to include this particular story in this book to show you that no one and nothing can take away our life without God's knowledge and permission. Once our lives belong to Him, He becomes the watchman and the keeper of them.

About 4:00 p.m. on Christmas Day of 2004, I was driving through the "Loup Loup Pass" in North Central Washington. Snow had begun falling earlier that day and by the time I reached the top of the pass, the roads were completely covered. I was listening to music and thinking about a chapter of my new book when my car began to slide on the icy snow. Immediately, all four of my wheels locked up. Looking ahead, I saw that I was headed for a sharp curve with 200-foot drop-off on my left. I tried to push the gas and then the brake while jerking the wheel to the right so I could make the curve without going into the oncoming traffic. My car picked up speed rapidly, exceeding 60 mph. My front wheels would not unlock and I continued to slide for what seemed like an eternity. I slid into the opposite lane of traffic, headed straight for the cliff. If a car had been coming at that moment, we would have collided.

It's amazing how many different thoughts can cross your mind in just a few seconds. For me it seemed more like minutes as my car, completely out of my control, jumped over the small curb along the edge of the road and headed down the cliff. If my car rolled over, I would either die or be seriously injured. I thought, "Am I going to die? Is this it?" But then I said to myself, "No, I can't die, it's Christmas today, and I have much more to do!" There was not much time to say anything else but, "Lord, please save me."

I hit the brakes one last time. My wheels unlocked, and my right back tire got stuck into three or four inches of dirt and extra asphalt. Both of my left wheels were hanging and the front right was barely touching the ground. I believe that God's angels held my car for the next two-and-a-half hours before I was pulled out. The police, the tow truck, and everyone who stopped to help me were amazed that I was alive. I was completely unhurt, and my car didn't even have a scratch. It was Christmas day, and I had one of the greatest opportunities to share Jesus with each one of these individuals. A police officer escorted me on to my destination, where I arrived completely unharmed.

Later that night, lying in my bed, I thanked God for saving my life and for the opportunity to tell those who didn't know Him of His goodness and love. God turns every trap of the enemy into an amazing testimony for His glory!

DAY 18

Perfect Love

Her eyes began to swell up with tears of overwhelming joy. It was her first time to wrap her arms around the tiny body of her newborn baby boy. The exhausting journey from Nazareth to Bethlehem had been exchanged with a promise that was now reality. The rejection, the shame, and the pain in her heart and body were quickly replaced with a greater hope, a greater fulfillment, and a greater love.

As she gazed at the closed eyes of her son, a few memories from the past slipped into her thoughts. It seemed like yesterday, while in her preparation to be married to Joseph, she encountered the angel of the Lord. A visit she would never be able to forget. She was a young, virgin woman, chosen by God to become the mother of His Son, Jesus. In spite of the fear of the unknown, and the inability to understand how everything would come to pass, she simply chose to obey. For nine months after the angel Gabriel visited her, there was a cost to be counted, a responsibility to be weighed, and a determination for endurance to be found.

Her pursuit of obedience had paid off. He was here! The Messiah, the Savior of the world, was born! The One, who had given her life, had become flesh and blood and was now sleeping tightly in her arms. What an honor, what a privilege to be the first one to hold the Savior. Her heart was singing praises accompanied by angels and all of creation, humbly bowing in worship and adoration before the living Lord.

A perfect gift, a perfect love, expressed to us through God's only Son - Jesus Christ. Even though He came for us all, He continues to come to each of us individually. Just like Mary, at one point in our lives we face an opportunity to hold the Savior of the world, by accepting Him into our hearts and allowing Him to become a part of our lives.

The cold, dirty manger where Jesus was born that night didn't stay dark and unnoticed for very long. Christ came to a world of darkness; He came to a place where fear and hatred rule through the pollution of sin. However, His love outshines the darkness, overrules the fear, and cleanses us from all guilt and shame. Mary and Joseph understood their responsibility—they couldn't have Jesus only for themselves. They had to share Him with others.

Love is made perfect only when given to those in need. Once we have discovered that love, once we have found the Messiah, Emmanuel, we have a responsibility—to share Him with those who do not know Him.

Let's never forget to give away the most important gift of all, the perfect gift and the perfect love found only in Jesus Christ.

DAY 19

Motivated by the impossible

It was nearly 8:00 pm on Friday night, December the 19th, 2004 and just a few days before Christmas. As I watched people walk in and out of stores and rush to catch the subway in Brooklyn, it appeared as though the ghetto of New York City was just waking up to a typical December morning rather than winding down its day. However, the night was wearing on, as the sun had been down for a few hours. Darkness slowly cast its creepy shadow over the corners of the streets. Life carried on, even late at night, but the sense of danger permeated the air. I was out with one of the workers from Metro Ministries delivering Christmas presents to the kids who attend the Saturday Sunday School.

Although this was my second Christmas Holiday to make home visitations in the ghetto, seeing the excitement in the children's eyes and the precious smiles on their faces was definitely not a "second-hand" experience. And there was more in store! This was a night unlike any other; it was my night to meet the child that I personally sponsor—Cary, a six-year-old boy, who lives with his mom.

Walking up to their apartment, I noticed their door was held shut with only a thin metal wire. The door knob was missing. The lights in the apartment were out, indicating that both he and his mom were not at home. I left the apartment determined not to give up. This night would be the only opportunity for us to meet each other on my trip.

After a few hours passed, we decided to drive over to his grandmother's apartment. The front eight-foot fence door was locked. Desperate to find him, I climbed over the fence and rang the doorbell—another fruitless effort. Upon our return to the van, we prayed that God would help us find Cary's mom. Within five minutes, we saw her walking down the street. That's right—our mission was accomplished!

Perhaps a gift or a home visitation doesn't seem like a big deal to some people, but to Cary and his mom, it was the best Christmas present they had ever received. They were just two of over 45,000 lives that were touched in only seven days by Metro workers and volunteers. We gave all the children a Christmas gift and shared Jesus with them and their families. It seems almost impossible if you really think about it.

Have you ever asked yourself the question, "What causes people to carry on, when the road of life seems difficult and even hopelessly impossible?" I believe the word impossible itself holds the answer. When challenged to put our trust in God, we can achieve the unattainable. This is a time to live our lives motivated by the impossible!

⟡DAY 20⟡

Jesus our true shepherd

"The Lord is my shepherd. I have everything I need..."

Psalms 23:1 TLB

Late one rainy night on my way home to Seattle, I was enjoying my time alone with God, meditating on His word, and going over the ministry events that had transpired that weekend. My heart was so overwhelmed with God's love that I really couldn't find the right words to express my emotions and gratitude to Him.

Then, mixed with the rejoicing in my spirit, I noticed a deep sense of unrest in my heart. My soul was not at ease. I felt a bit of heaviness mixed with fear. How could two opposing emotions surface simultaneously? Perhaps we all have felt that way at times.

Because I did not know the source of my anxieties, or perhaps unspoken wants, I decided to take a moment to review the recent events in my life. Less than five minutes later my thoughts confronted God's truth, exposing my humanness like so many times before. The gentle whisper of the Holy Spirit wrapped my troubled heart in a warm blanket of peace. "The human soul and spirit long for a shepherd," He said, "someone to guide the way, provide rest, food, and protection when harm and opposition come, and love without condition or hidden agenda."

Many times the problems and obstacles around us become our "shepherds." The voices of fear, helplessness, disaster, and problems resonate more loudly than the voice of the true Shepherd. Soon we begin to follow their lead and find ourselves tricked not into a place of green pastures and still waters, but rather in a place of anxieties, worries, depression and doubt.

When God is not allowed to be a shepherd in certain areas of our heart and life, someone or something else takes the lead. It could be us, the enemy, or an external circumstance. Anything outside of Christ creates more wants and only brings dissatisfaction. Only when Christ is the shepherd can every want, desire, and need be completely met.

The enemy has no power over the areas where Christ leads us as our shepherd. As a shepherd, Christ is the doorkeeper of our hearts and the watchman over our lives. He never falls asleep, and He doesn't allow anything or anyone to enter our life without His knowledge. He is before us, with us, and around us. We will never be in want or lack, and we'll have all that we need. But the key question is, "Is Christ our shepherd?"

~~~ DAY 21 ~~~

Thankful

Luke 17:11-19

Luke 17:15 "One of them, when he saw he was healed, came back, praising God in a loud voice. 16. He threw himself at Jesus' feet and thanked Him—and he was a Samaritan. 17. Jesus asked, "Were not all ten cleansed? Where are the other nine?""

Emotional and physical exhaustion began to take over as our small, ragged group approached Jerusalem. Desperate from the rejection and isolation of our disease, we had learned to accept the hopelessness that leprosy brings. How I despised the loathing stares of others as we passed their way. As social outcasts, no one dared to come near us or speak to us.

But that day, we saw Jesus walking in the distance. A ray of hope flashed within us as we cried out in a loud voice, "Jesus, Master, have mercy on us." He saw us! But His look was different. Not like anything we had experienced from others. A quick gaze into His eyes was all we needed to feel compassion, acceptance, and love. "Go and show yourselves to the priests." His words were few, but spoken with such authority that faith stirred within our hearts.

We obeyed Him and went on our way. Covered in dust from the long journey, I had not seen my sores for a long time. For a moment I allowed myself to imagine what it would feel like to be free from my shameful disease. As I continued with the other nine, I sensed a change in my body. In order to take a closer look, I stopped to brush off the dirt. With every stroke I made in removing the filth, my heart began to beat faster and my eyes couldn't believe what I discovered. I was no longer a leper! My skin was clear and I was healed! I was not the only one. The others were healed as well!

I had to return to Jesus. I had to thank Him for the miracle. I couldn't just keep going on my way. I ran back so fast, it felt as though my feet weren't touching the ground. There was Jesus, still walking! I threw myself down, alone at His feet. All I could offer Him was a grateful heart. He had given me a new beginning, a new life. He was the only One that was worthy of my praise.

How many times do we continue on our way of business, stress, or worries of life, and never take the time to notice the miracles that God performs for us? All it takes is to stop, look, and shake off "the dust" that covers the blessings He has given us. A heart filled with gratitude and thankfulness is all that Jesus is waiting for. Will you be the one who returns?

PRAYER OF SALVATION

Accepting Jesus in your heart is the most important decision you will ever make in your life. It's a choice that will have influence not only on your earthly life, but it will also determine where you spend eternity. If God has touched your heart, while reading this book and you realize that you have never made Jesus your personal Lord and Savior, now is your opportunity! God can change your life today, the same way He changed mine! He wants to love you and help you. If you believe that Jesus is the ONLY true God and want Him to come into your heart today, please, read this prayer out loud:

"Dear Lord Jesus, I acknowledge You as the ONLY true God, through whom I can obtain salvation and receive forgiveness. I repent for all of my sins and ask You to forgive me and to cleanse me with Your blood. Please, come into my heart and be my Lord and Savior. Fill me with your Holy Spirit and help me to live for You. I chose to serve you and to obey You for the rest of my life! In the Name of Jesus! Amen!"

If you prayed this prayer, I want you to know that now you are no longer alone. Jesus lives in your heart and He will be your best friend. Don't be afraid to call on Him!

ABOUT THE AUTHOR

Ceitci Demirkova was born and raised in Bulgaria, a former Communist country. After the fall of the Communist regime in 1989, at age 16 Ceitci heard the Gospel and accepted Jesus into her heart. Not long after she became a Christian, God spoke to her that she would one day travel and preach His word to people from all nations. In January of 1995 she was accepted as a student at Victory Bible Institute in Tulsa, OK. She began full time ministry shortly before graduation.

Ceitci Demirkova Ministries is a non-profit organization started in July 1996. Verdigris Valley Christian Fellowship (former Greater New Life Church) in Altoona, KS functions as her service agency provider. Today, Ceitci is a licensed and ordained minister (Victory Christian Center, Tulsa, OK and Verdigris Valley Christian Fellowship, Altoona, KS) who travels across America and the world preaching and teaching God's Word.

Her vision is Jesus and her passion is to know Him and to make Him known to others!

TO ORDER MORE COPIES OF THIS BOOK, PLEASE CONTACT:

Ceitci Demirkova Ministries
PO Box 126
Altoona, KS 66710

Ph (206) 852-8810

info@ceitci.org

Other publications by Ceitci Demirkova

"If You Have God You Have Everything"
A Faith Adventure Of A Young Bulgarian Woman

To order, visit: www.ceitci.org

FOR MINISTRY INFORMATION WRITE OR CALL:

Ceitci Demirkova
PO Box 126
Altoona, KS 66710

Ph (206) 852-8810

www.ceitci.org

info@ceitci.org

Please include your prayer requests and comments when you write.